If Found, Please Return to

....

....

....

The FIVE-MINUTE JOURNAL

for **KIDS**

By Intelligent Change

Illustrated by Nina Popovska

GET IN TOUCH
hello@intelligentchange.com

CREATED BY
The Intelligent Change Team

Published by Intelligent Change LLC.
ISBN 9780991846245
3rd Print Run

©2020 Intelligent Change. All rights reserved. All material in this journal may not be reproduced, transmitted or distributed in any form without the written permission of Intelligent Change LLC.

While the publisher has used their best efforts in preparing this journal, they make no representations or warranties with respect to the accuracy or completeness of the contents of this journal. The advice and strategies contained herein may not be suitable for your situation. You should consult with a professional where appropriate. Neither the publisher nor authors shall be liable for any loss of profit or any other commercial damages, including but not limited to special, incidental, consequential, or other damages.

Designed by Florencia Baldini
Printed in China

Intelligent Change
www.intelligentchange.com

Dedication

To the childlike wonder that exists within us all and helps us live with more joy, meaning, and purpose.

Those who don't believe in magic will never find it.

— ROALD DAHL

Contents

A Toothbrush for Your Mind... Ready to Smile?	6
How to Use this Journal	8
The Magic of Gratitude	10
A Great Day!	12
A Superhero in Each of Us	14
Finding the Good in Each Day	16
Always Keep Learning	18
Challenges	20
Word of the Day	21
Putting it all together	22
The Journal	26
Woo hoo! Way to go!	210

A Toothbrush for Your Mind

The Five Minute Journal is like a toothbrush for your mind. You use it every morning and night. Writing in your Five Minute Journal keeps your mind fresh and happy, just like brushing your teeth keeps your mouth clean and ready to smile.

When you write in your Five Minute Journal, you train your mind to focus on the good things in your life such as your family, friends, or your super cozy bed. This helps your mind be more friendly and slowly, but surely, worrisome thoughts will disappear.

Ready to begin your Five Minute Journal adventure? *Let's go!*

How to Use this Journal

- [ ] Keep it near your bed with your favorite pen, pencil, or crayon
- [ ] Fill out the morning section as soon as you wake up
- [ ] Fill out the night section before going to bed
- [ ] Repeat daily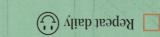

The Magic of Gratitude

Olivia begins every morning writing what she is grateful for in her Five Minute Journal. She closes her eyes and thinks about the things she is thankful for in her life. When she feels a warm, happy feeling in her heart, she has decided what to write. Today she writes she is grateful for her mom's laugh.

What are you grateful for?

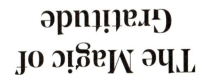

A Great Day!

After Benny writes what he is grateful for in his Five Minute Journal, he thinks about what would make his day great. Benny imagines himself during the day and writes:
"I will play with my friends during recess."
This will make Benny's day great!

What would make your day great?

Daily Affirmation I am...

Inside each of us lives a inner voice. Our inner voice can be directed to inspire us and make us feel like our strongest self by repeating a daily affirmation. Daily affirmations define who you want to be. Think of them like a daily motto.

Olivia's daily affirmation is,
"I am healthy, strong, and energetic."

Benny's daily affirmation is,
"I am kind to everyone I meet."

What is your daily affirmation?

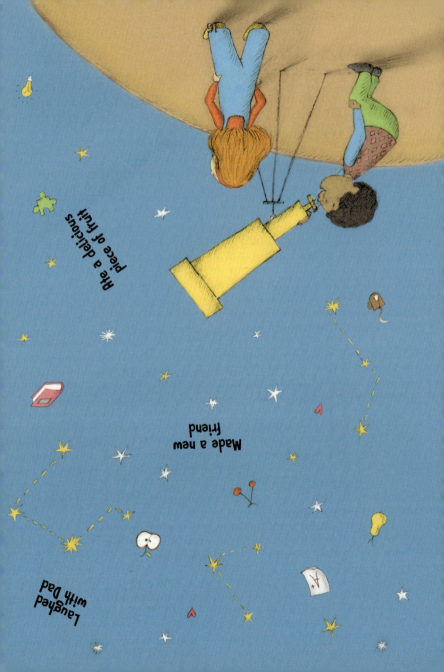

Finding the Good in Each Day

Benny and Olivia's favorite part of the day is thinking about all the positive things that happened. A friend's kind words, learning something new, and eating delicious fruit. Without reflecting back on your day, it's too easy to forget these good things, and focus instead on things that maybe didn't go as planned. It is like holding a mirror to look back on your day.

What amazing things happened to you today?

Always Keep Learning

When Olivia's mom asks her what she learned today, Olivia scratches her head and says "nothing" because she cannot remember. Her mom persists, "dig deeper". After more reflection, Olivia says she learned that a group of cats are called a clowder and she loves drawing. With just a little extra thought, she found a lesson from her day.

What did you learn today?

19

Challenges

On certain days of the week, Benny finds a challenge in his Five Minute Journal. These challenges help inspire Benny to be more confident and positive. From kind deeds to spontaneous dancing, this is how growth happens. When Benny gets stuck he asks his parents for help. Most importantly, Benny has a whole lot of fun tackling his challenges!

Word of the Day

Today, Olivia learns that "gratitude" means a feeling of appreciation and thankfulness. Gratitude is the word of the day presented in her Five Minute Journal. By learning a new word each day, Olivia adds to her communication toolbox. This helps her express herself and be better understood by others.

What new word will YOU learn today?"

Putting it
All Together

Congratulations! You have just learned how to use the Five Minute Journal. Now is when your journey REALLY begins. Committing to writing in this journal for just 5 days will help you stick with it for a really long time.

COMMITTING TO THE HABIT

I _____ Olivia _____ ,

commit to writing in The Five Minute Journal for at least

5 days in a row, starting __7__ / __5__ / 20 __18__ .

Writing in this journal is important to me because:

__I want to learn about my thoughts.__

If I finish 5 days of writing in this journal, I will reward
myself with:

__Watching my favorite movie.__

I will do the following to ensure I do The Five Minute
Journal every day:

- ☒ Keep The Five Minute Journal by my bedside
- ☒ Do The Five Minute Journal after waking up
- ☒ Do The Five Minute Journal before going to sleep
- ☒ Ask my parents for help if I get stuck

FILL IN THE BLANKS ↓

I _____ ,
commit to writing in The Five Minute Journal for at least
5 days in a row, starting ____ / ____ / 20____ .

Writing in this journal is important to me because:

_____

If I finish 5 days of writing in this journal, I will reward
myself with:

_____

I will do the following to ensure I do The Five Minute
Journal every day:

☐ Keep The Five Minute Journal by my bedside

☐ Do The Five Minute Journal after waking up

☐ Do The Five Minute Journal before going to sleep

☐ Ask my parents for help if I get stuck

Let's begin!

The
Journal

DATE __7__ / __5__ /20 __18__

*Don't cry because it's over, smile
because it happened.*

— DR. SEUSS

I AM GRATEFUL FOR...

My Mom's laugh

WHAT WOULD MAKE TODAY GREAT?

Playing with my friends during recess

DAILY AFFIRMATION. I AM...

I am healthy and strong

ONE AMAZING THING THAT HAPPENED TODAY

Walking to school with dad

WHAT DID I LEARN TODAY?

A group of cats are called a clowder

DATE _____ / _____ / 20 _____

Adventure is worthwhile in itself.
— AMELIA EARHART

 I AM GRATEFUL FOR...

WHAT WOULD MAKE TODAY GREAT?

DAILY AFFIRMATION. I AM...

 ONE AMAZING THING THAT HAPPENED TODAY

WHAT DID I LEARN TODAY?

DATE _____ / _____ / 20 _____

WORD OF THE DAY: **Gratitude**

A feeling of appreciation or thanks.

I AM GRATEFUL FOR...

_____

WHAT WOULD MAKE TODAY GREAT?

_____

DAILY AFFIRMATION. I AM...

_____

ONE AMAZING THING THAT HAPPENED TODAY

_____

WHAT DID I LEARN TODAY?

_____

DATE _____ / _____ / 20 _____

Yesterday is history. Tomorrow is
a mystery. Today is a gift. That's
why we call it 'The Present'.

– ALICE MORSE EARLE

I AM GRATEFUL FOR...

WHAT WOULD MAKE TODAY GREAT?

DAILY AFFIRMATION. I AM...

ONE AMAZING THING THAT HAPPENED TODAY

WHAT DID I LEARN TODAY?

DATE _____ / _____ / 20 _____

You've got to do your own growing, no matter
how tall your grandfather was.

– IRISH PROVERB

I AM GRATEFUL FOR...

WHAT WOULD MAKE TODAY GREAT?

DAILY AFFIRMATION. I AM...

ONE AMAZING THING THAT HAPPENED TODAY

WHAT DID I LEARN TODAY?

DATE _____ / _____ / 20 _____

We make a living by what we get,
but we make a life by what we give.
– WINSTON CHURCHILL

I AM GRATEFUL FOR...

_____

WHAT WOULD MAKE TODAY GREAT?

_____

DAILY AFFIRMATION. I AM...

_____

ONE AMAZING THING THAT HAPPENED TODAY

_____

WHAT DID I LEARN TODAY?

_____

Congratulations, 5 Days Finished!

Congratulations! You have just committed to five days of sticking with The Five Minute Journal. You have taken an important step to stick with this journal for a long time. Now it's time to reward yourself. Flip back to page 25 to see what you wrote down and enjoy!

DATE _____ / _____ / 20 _____

WORD OF THE DAY: Respect

A feeling of admiring someone or something
that is good, valuable, important, etc.

 I AM GRATEFUL FOR...

_____

WHAT WOULD MAKE TODAY GREAT?

_____

DAILY AFFIRMATION. I AM...

_____

ONE AMAZING THING THAT HAPPENED TODAY

_____

WHAT DID I LEARN TODAY?

_____

34

DATE _____ / _____ / 20 _____

························· CHALLENGE ·························

Laugh for 10 seconds.

I AM GRATEFUL FOR...

WHAT WOULD MAKE TODAY GREAT?

DAILY AFFIRMATION. I AM...

ONE AMAZING THING THAT HAPPENED TODAY

WHAT DID I LEARN TODAY?

DATE _____ / _____ / 20 _____

We grow great by dreams.
– WOODROW WILSON

 I AM GRATEFUL FOR...

WHAT WOULD MAKE TODAY GREAT?

DAILY AFFIRMATION. I AM...

ONE AMAZING THING THAT HAPPENED TODAY

WHAT DID I LEARN TODAY?

DATE _____ / _____ / 20 _____

WORD OF THE DAY: Kind

Having or showing a desire to help others;
wanting and liking to do good things that bring
happiness to others.

I AM GRATEFUL FOR...

_____

WHAT WOULD MAKE TODAY GREAT?

_____

DAILY AFFIRMATION. I AM...

_____

ONE AMAZING THING THAT HAPPENED TODAY

_____

WHAT DID I LEARN TODAY?

_____

DATE _____ / _____ / 20 _____

Life is a succession of lessons
which must be lived to be understood.

– HELEN KELLER

 I AM GRATEFUL FOR...

WHAT WOULD MAKE TODAY GREAT?

DAILY AFFIRMATION. I AM...

ONE AMAZING THING THAT HAPPENED TODAY

WHAT DID I LEARN TODAY?

DATE _____ / _____ / 20 _____

We all can dance when we find music we love.
— GILES ANDREAE

I AM GRATEFUL FOR...

WHAT WOULD MAKE TODAY GREAT?

DAILY AFFIRMATION. I AM...

ONE AMAZING THING THAT HAPPENED TODAY

WHAT DID I LEARN TODAY?

DATE ____ / ____ / 20 ____

Don't let what you can't do stop you from
doing what you can do.

— JOHN WOODEN

I AM GRATEFUL FOR...

WHAT WOULD MAKE TODAY GREAT?

DAILY AFFIRMATION. I AM...

ONE AMAZING THING THAT HAPPENED TODAY

WHAT DID I LEARN TODAY?

40

DATE ___ / ___ / 20 ___

WORD OF THE DAY: Consideration
Careful thought; sensitivity towards others.

I AM GRATEFUL FOR...

_____

WHAT WOULD MAKE TODAY GREAT?

_____

DAILY AFFIRMATION. I AM...

_____

ONE AMAZING THING THAT HAPPENED TODAY

_____

WHAT DID I LEARN TODAY?

_____

DATE ___ / ___ / 20 ___

---- CHALLENGE ----
Give a friend a high-five.

☀ I AM GRATEFUL FOR...

WHAT WOULD MAKE TODAY GREAT?

DAILY AFFIRMATION. I AM...

☾ ONE AMAZING THING THAT HAPPENED TODAY

WHAT DID I LEARN TODAY?

DATE _____ / _____ / 20 _____

You have brains in your head. You have feet in your
shoes. You can steer yourself any direction you choose.
You're on your own. And you know what you know. And
YOU are the one who'll decide where to go...

– DR. SEUSS

I AM GRATEFUL FOR...

WHAT WOULD MAKE TODAY GREAT?

DAILY AFFIRMATION. I AM...

ONE AMAZING THING THAT HAPPENED TODAY

WHAT DID I LEARN TODAY?

DATE _____ / _____ / 20 _____

WORD OF THE DAY: Engaging

Very interesting or pleasing in a way
that holds your attention.

 I AM GRATEFUL FOR...

_____

WHAT WOULD MAKE TODAY GREAT?

_____

DAILY AFFIRMATION. I AM...

_____

ONE AMAZING THING THAT HAPPENED TODAY

_____

WHAT DID I LEARN TODAY?

_____

DATE _____ / _____ / 20 _____

Make each day your masterpiece.
– JOHN WOODEN

I AM GRATEFUL FOR...

_____

WHAT WOULD MAKE TODAY GREAT?

_____

DAILY AFFIRMATION. I AM...

_____

ONE AMAZING THING THAT HAPPENED TODAY

_____

WHAT DID I LEARN TODAY?

_____

DATE _____ / _____ / 20 _____

It's not what happens to you,
but how you react to it that matters.

– EPICTETUS

 I AM GRATEFUL FOR...

_____

WHAT WOULD MAKE TODAY GREAT?

_____

DAILY AFFIRMATION. I AM...

_____

ONE AMAZING THING THAT HAPPENED TODAY

_____

WHAT DID I LEARN TODAY?

_____

DATE _____ / _____ / 20 _____

If you can dream it, you can do it.
– TOM FITZGERALD

I AM GRATEFUL FOR...

_____

WHAT WOULD MAKE TODAY GREAT?

_____

DAILY AFFIRMATION. I AM...

_____

ONE AMAZING THING THAT HAPPENED TODAY

_____

WHAT DID I LEARN TODAY?

_____

DATE _____ / _____ / 20 _____

WORD OF THE DAY: **Share**

To let someone else have or use a part of something.

 I AM GRATEFUL FOR...

_____

WHAT WOULD MAKE TODAY GREAT?

_____

DAILY AFFIRMATION. I AM...

_____

 ONE AMAZING THING THAT HAPPENED TODAY

_____

WHAT DID I LEARN TODAY?

_____

DATE ____ / ____ / 20 ____

.... CHALLENGE ....
What do you want to be when you grow up?
I want to be _____.

I AM GRATEFUL FOR...

_____

WHAT WOULD MAKE TODAY GREAT?

_____

DAILY AFFIRMATION. I AM...

_____

ONE AMAZING THING THAT HAPPENED TODAY

_____

WHAT DID I LEARN TODAY?

_____

DATE ____ / ____ / 20 ____

No one is perfect — that's why pencils have erasers.

– **WOLFGANG RIEBE**

I AM GRATEFUL FOR...

_____

WHAT WOULD MAKE TODAY GREAT?

_____

DAILY AFFIRMATION. I AM...

_____

🌙 ONE AMAZING THING THAT HAPPENED TODAY

_____

WHAT DID I LEARN TODAY?

_____

50

DATE _____ / _____ / 20 _____

WORD OF THE DAY: **Love**
A strong feeling of affection.

I AM GRATEFUL FOR...

_____

WHAT WOULD MAKE TODAY GREAT?

_____

DAILY AFFIRMATION. I AM...

_____

ONE AMAZING THING THAT HAPPENED TODAY

_____

WHAT DID I LEARN TODAY?

_____

51

DATE _____ / _____ / 20 _____

*Only surround yourself with people
who will lift you higher.*

– OPRAH WINFREY

 I AM GRATEFUL FOR...

_____

WHAT WOULD MAKE TODAY GREAT?

_____

DAILY AFFIRMATION. I AM...

_____

ONE AMAZING THING THAT HAPPENED TODAY

_____

WHAT DID I LEARN TODAY?

_____

DATE _____ / _____ / 20 _____

Anything is possible. Anything can be.
— SHEL SILVERSTEIN

I AM GRATEFUL FOR...

_____

WHAT WOULD MAKE TODAY GREAT?

_____

DAILY AFFIRMATION. I AM...

_____

ONE AMAZING THING THAT HAPPENED TODAY

_____

WHAT DID I LEARN TODAY?

_____

53

DATE _____ / _____ / 20 _____

When one door of happiness closes, another
opens; but often we look so long at the closed
door that we do not see the one that
has been opened for us.

– HELEN KELLER

 I AM GRATEFUL FOR...

WHAT WOULD MAKE TODAY GREAT?

DAILY AFFIRMATION. I AM...

ONE AMAZING THING THAT HAPPENED TODAY

WHAT DID I LEARN TODAY?

DATE / / 20

WORD OF THE DAY: *Mindfulness*

Maintaining a moment-by-moment awareness of our thoughts, feelings, bodily sensations, and surrounding environment.

I AM GRATEFUL FOR...

_____

WHAT WOULD MAKE TODAY GREAT?

_____

DAILY AFFIRMATION. I AM...

_____

ONE AMAZING THING THAT HAPPENED TODAY

_____

WHAT DID I LEARN TODAY?

_____

55

DATE _____ / _____ / 20 _____

········· **CHALLENGE** ·········

Say something nice to your classmate today.

 I AM GRATEFUL FOR...

_____

WHAT WOULD MAKE TODAY GREAT?

_____

DAILY AFFIRMATION. I AM...

_____

ONE AMAZING THING THAT HAPPENED TODAY

_____

WHAT DID I LEARN TODAY?

_____

DATE ———— / ———— / 20 ————

Be kind whenever possible. It
is always possible.
- TIBETAN SAYING

I AM GRATEFUL FOR...

WHAT WOULD MAKE TODAY GREAT?

DAILY AFFIRMATION. I AM...

ONE AMAZING THING THAT HAPPENED TODAY

WHAT DID I LEARN TODAY?

DATE _____ / _____ / 20 _____

WORD OF THE DAY: Compassion

A feeling of sympathy and concern for another person's suffering that leads to a desire to help.

 I AM GRATEFUL FOR...

WHAT WOULD MAKE TODAY GREAT?

DAILY AFFIRMATION. I AM...

ONE AMAZING THING THAT HAPPENED TODAY

WHAT DID I LEARN TODAY?

DATE ____ / ____ / 20 ____

Three things cannot be long hidden:
the sun, the moon, and the truth.
- BUDDHA -

I AM GRATEFUL FOR...

WHAT WOULD MAKE TODAY GREAT?

DAILY AFFIRMATION. I AM...

ONE AMAZING THING THAT HAPPENED TODAY

WHAT DID I LEARN TODAY?

DATE ____ / ____ / 20 ____

Why fit in when you were born to stand out?
- DR. SEUSS

 I AM GRATEFUL FOR...

WHAT WOULD MAKE TODAY GREAT?

DAILY AFFIRMATION. I AM...

ONE AMAZING THING THAT HAPPENED TODAY

WHAT DID I LEARN TODAY?

DATE _____ / _____ / 20 _____

Mix a little foolishness with your serious
plans. It is lovely to be silly at the
right moment.

– HORACE

I AM GRATEFUL FOR...

WHAT WOULD MAKE TODAY GREAT?

DAILY AFFIRMATION. I AM...

ONE AMAZING THING THAT HAPPENED TODAY

WHAT DID I LEARN TODAY?

DATE _____ / _____ / 20 _____

WORD OF THE DAY: **Optimism**

A feeling or belief that good things will happen in the future; a feeling or belief that what you hope for will happen.

 I AM GRATEFUL FOR...

WHAT WOULD MAKE TODAY GREAT?

DAILY AFFIRMATION. I AM...

 ONE AMAZING THING THAT HAPPENED TODAY

WHAT DID I LEARN TODAY?

DATE _____ / _____ / 20 _____

······· CHALLENGE ·······

Draw your own superhero today.

I AM GRATEFUL FOR...

WHAT WOULD MAKE TODAY GREAT?

DAILY AFFIRMATION. I AM...

ONE AMAZING THING THAT HAPPENED TODAY

WHAT DID I LEARN TODAY?

DATE _____ / _____ / 20 _____

The moment you doubt whether you can fly,
you cease forever to be able to do it.

- PETER PAN

I AM GRATEFUL FOR...

WHAT WOULD MAKE TODAY GREAT?

DAILY AFFIRMATION. I AM...

ONE AMAZING THING THAT HAPPENED TODAY

WHAT DID I LEARN TODAY?

DATE _____ / _____ / 20 _____

WORD OF THE DAY: Meditation

To reflect quietly and observe your own
thoughts to gain clarity and peace.

I AM GRATEFUL FOR...

_____

WHAT WOULD MAKE TODAY GREAT?

_____

DAILY AFFIRMATION. I AM...

_____

ONE AMAZING THING THAT HAPPENED TODAY

_____

WHAT DID I LEARN TODAY?

_____

DATE _____ / _____ / 20 _____

Promise me you'll remember, you are
BRAVER than you believe, STRONGER than you
seem, SMARTER than you think.

- A.A. MILNE

 I AM GRATEFUL FOR...

_____

WHAT WOULD MAKE TODAY GREAT?

_____

DAILY AFFIRMATION. I AM...

_____

ONE AMAZING THING THAT HAPPENED TODAY

_____

WHAT DID I LEARN TODAY?

_____

DATE _____ / _____ / 20 _____

If you have good thoughts they will shine out of your face like sunbeams and you will always look lovely.

- ROALD DAHL

I AM GRATEFUL FOR...

_____

WHAT WOULD MAKE TODAY GREAT?

_____

DAILY AFFIRMATION. I AM...

_____

ONE AMAZING THING THAT HAPPENED TODAY

_____

WHAT DID I LEARN TODAY?

_____

DATE _____ / _____ / 20 _____

In every job that must be done, there is an element of fun. You find the fun, and the job's a game.

- MARY POPPINS

 I AM GRATEFUL FOR...

_____

WHAT WOULD MAKE TODAY GREAT?

_____

DAILY AFFIRMATION. I AM...

_____

ONE AMAZING THING THAT HAPPENED TODAY

_____

WHAT DID I LEARN TODAY?

_____

DATE _____ / _____ / 20 _____

WORD OF THE DAY: **Persevere**

Continuing to try to do something even though it is difficult.

I AM GRATEFUL FOR...

_____

WHAT WOULD MAKE TODAY GREAT?

_____

DAILY AFFIRMATION. I AM...

_____

ONE AMAZING THING THAT HAPPENED TODAY

_____

WHAT DID I LEARN TODAY?

_____

DATE _____ / _____ / 20 _____

······· **CHALLENGE** ·······

Dance for 10 seconds right now.

I AM GRATEFUL FOR...

WHAT WOULD MAKE TODAY GREAT?

DAILY AFFIRMATION. I AM...

ONE AMAZING THING THAT HAPPENED TODAY

WHAT DID I LEARN TODAY?

DATE _____ / _____ / 20 _____

Winning doesn't always mean being first.
Winning means you're doing better than
you've done before.

- BONNIE BLAIR

I AM GRATEFUL FOR...

_____

WHAT WOULD MAKE TODAY GREAT?

_____

DAILY AFFIRMATION. I AM...

_____

ONE AMAZING THING THAT HAPPENED TODAY

_____

WHAT DID I LEARN TODAY?

_____

DATE _____ / _____ / 20 _____

WORD OF THE DAY: Dedicated

Being committed to and loyal to
someone or something.

I AM GRATEFUL FOR...

WHAT WOULD MAKE TODAY GREAT?

DAILY AFFIRMATION. I AM...

ONE AMAZING THING THAT HAPPENED TODAY

WHAT DID I LEARN TODAY?

DATE _____ / _____ / 20 _____

Your story may not have such a happy
beginning but that does not make you who you
are, it is the rest of it — who you choose to be

- SOOTHSAYER (KUNG FU PANDA 2)

I AM GRATEFUL FOR...

_____

WHAT WOULD MAKE TODAY GREAT?

_____

DAILY AFFIRMATION. I AM...

_____

ONE AMAZING THING THAT HAPPENED TODAY

_____

WHAT DID I LEARN TODAY?

_____

DATE _____ / _____ / 20 _____

The more that you read, the more things you will know. The more that you learn, the more places you'll go.

- DR. SEUSS

 I AM GRATEFUL FOR...

WHAT WOULD MAKE TODAY GREAT?

DAILY AFFIRMATION. I AM...

ONE AMAZING THING THAT HAPPENED TODAY

WHAT DID I LEARN TODAY?

DATE _____ / _____ / 20 _____

Life will never be the same because there had
never been anyone like YOU ever in the world.
– NANCY TILLMAN

I AM GRATEFUL FOR...

_____

WHAT WOULD MAKE TODAY GREAT?

_____

DAILY AFFIRMATION. I AM...

_____

ONE AMAZING THING THAT HAPPENED TODAY

_____

WHAT DID I LEARN TODAY?

_____

DATE _____ / _____ / 20 _____

WORD OF THE DAY: Spontaneous

Being open to things that have not been planned; sometimes impulsive.

 I AM GRATEFUL FOR...

_____

WHAT WOULD MAKE TODAY GREAT?

_____

DAILY AFFIRMATION. I AM...

_____

 ONE AMAZING THING THAT HAPPENED TODAY

_____

WHAT DID I LEARN TODAY?

_____

DATE ____ / ____ / 20 ____

.... CHALLENGE ....
Help your parents cook a meal today.
....

I AM GRATEFUL FOR...

_____

WHAT WOULD MAKE TODAY GREAT?

_____

DAILY AFFIRMATION. I AM...

_____

ONE AMAZING THING THAT HAPPENED TODAY

_____

WHAT DID I LEARN TODAY?

_____

DATE _____ / _____ / 20 _____

"How do you spell 'LOVE'?" - Piglet
"You don't spell it, you feel it." -Pooh

- A.A. MILNE

I AM GRATEFUL FOR...

WHAT WOULD MAKE TODAY GREAT?

DAILY AFFIRMATION. I AM...

ONE AMAZING THING THAT HAPPENED TODAY

WHAT DID I LEARN TODAY?

DATE _____ / _____ / 20 _____

WORD OF THE DAY: Boldness

Being brave & confident; not afraid
to take risks.

I AM GRATEFUL FOR...

_____

WHAT WOULD MAKE TODAY GREAT?

_____

DAILY AFFIRMATION, I AM...

_____

ONE AMAZING THING THAT HAPPENED TODAY

_____

WHAT DID I LEARN TODAY?

_____

DATE _____ / _____ / 20 _____

Be yourself. Everyone else is already taken.
– OSCAR WILDE

 I AM GRATEFUL FOR...

_____

WHAT WOULD MAKE TODAY GREAT?

_____

DAILY AFFIRMATION. I AM...

_____

ONE AMAZING THING THAT HAPPENED TODAY

_____

WHAT DID I LEARN TODAY?

_____

DATE _____ / _____ / 20 _____

Courage doesn't always roar. Sometimes courage
is the quiet voice at the end of the day saying
I will try again tomorrow.

– MARY ANNE RADMACHER

I AM GRATEFUL FOR...

WHAT WOULD MAKE TODAY GREAT?

DAILY AFFIRMATION. I AM...

ONE AMAZING THING THAT HAPPENED TODAY

WHAT DID I LEARN TODAY?

DATE _____ / _____ / 20 _____

There are far better things ahead than
any we leave behind.

– C.S. LEWIS

 I AM GRATEFUL FOR...

WHAT WOULD MAKE TODAY GREAT?

DAILY AFFIRMATION. I AM...

ONE AMAZING THING THAT HAPPENED TODAY

WHAT DID I LEARN TODAY?

DATE _____ / _____ / 20 _____

WORD OF THE DAY: **Purpose**

The reason for which something is done or exists.

I AM GRATEFUL FOR...

_____

WHAT WOULD MAKE TODAY GREAT?

_____

DAILY AFFIRMATION. I AM...

_____

ONE AMAZING THING THAT HAPPENED TODAY

_____

WHAT DID I LEARN TODAY?

_____

DATE _____ / _____ / 20 _____

························· **CHALLENGE** ·························

Create a list of all your dreams. Write the date
on it and put it somewhere for safe keeping.

 I AM GRATEFUL FOR...

WHAT WOULD MAKE TODAY GREAT?

DAILY AFFIRMATION. I AM...

ONE AMAZING THING THAT HAPPENED TODAY

WHAT DID I LEARN TODAY?

DATE _____ / _____ / 20 _____

*It is our choices that show what we truly are,
far more than our abilities.*

– DUMBLEDORE (HARRY POTTER)

I AM GRATEFUL FOR...

WHAT WOULD MAKE TODAY GREAT?

DAILY AFFIRMATION. I AM...

ONE AMAZING THING THAT HAPPENED TODAY

WHAT DID I LEARN TODAY?

DATE _____ / _____ / 20 _____

WORD OF THE DAY: **Hero**

A person who is admired for great or brave acts or fine qualities.

 I AM GRATEFUL FOR...

_____

WHAT WOULD MAKE TODAY GREAT?

_____

DAILY AFFIRMATION. I AM...

_____

ONE AMAZING THING THAT HAPPENED TODAY

_____

WHAT DID I LEARN TODAY?

_____

DATE _____ / _____ / 20 _____

When something goes wrong in your life, just yell, "PLOT TWIST," and move on.

– MOLLY WEIS

I AM GRATEFUL FOR...

WHAT WOULD MAKE TODAY GREAT?

DAILY AFFIRMATION. I AM...

ONE AMAZING THING THAT HAPPENED TODAY

WHAT DID I LEARN TODAY?

DATE _____ / _____ / 20 _____

Wisdom begins in wonder.
– SOCRATES

 I AM GRATEFUL FOR...

WHAT WOULD MAKE TODAY GREAT?

DAILY AFFIRMATION. I AM...

ONE AMAZING THING THAT HAPPENED TODAY

WHAT DID I LEARN TODAY?

DATE _____ / _____ / 20 _____

Be curious, not judgmental.

– WALT WHITMAN

I AM GRATEFUL FOR...

WHAT WOULD MAKE TODAY GREAT?

DAILY AFFIRMATION. I AM...

ONE AMAZING THING THAT HAPPENED TODAY

WHAT DID I LEARN TODAY?

DATE _____ / _____ / 20 _____

WORD OF THE DAY: Motivate

To give yourself or someone a reason to do something; to stimulate enthusiasm to do something.

 I AM GRATEFUL FOR...

_____

WHAT WOULD MAKE TODAY GREAT?

_____

DAILY AFFIRMATION. I AM...

_____

ONE AMAZING THING THAT HAPPENED TODAY

_____

WHAT DID I LEARN TODAY?

_____

DATE ___/___/ 20___

---- CHALLENGE ----
Do 5 jumping jacks.

I AM GRATEFUL FOR...

WHAT WOULD MAKE TODAY GREAT?

DAILY AFFIRMATION. I AM...

ONE AMAZING THING THAT HAPPENED TODAY

WHAT DID I LEARN TODAY?

DATE ———— / ———— / 20 ————

If plan A didn't work, the alphabet
has 25 more letters.
— CLAIRE COOK

I AM GRATEFUL FOR...

WHAT WOULD MAKE TODAY GREAT?

DAILY AFFIRMATION. I AM...

ONE AMAZING THING THAT HAPPENED TODAY

WHAT DID I LEARN TODAY?

DATE ___ / ___ / 20 ___

WORD OF THE DAY: Productive
Working to produce or achieve a lot.

I AM GRATEFUL FOR...

___

WHAT WOULD MAKE TODAY GREAT?

___

DAILY AFFIRMATION, I AM...

___

ONE AMAZING THING THAT HAPPENED TODAY

___

WHAT DID I LEARN TODAY?

___

DATE _____ / _____ / 20 _____

*It's not about how badly you WANT something.
It's about what you are capable of!*

– CHIEF BOGO (ZOOTOPIA)

 I AM GRATEFUL FOR...

_____

WHAT WOULD MAKE TODAY GREAT?

_____

DAILY AFFIRMATION. I AM...

_____

 ONE AMAZING THING THAT HAPPENED TODAY

_____

WHAT DID I LEARN TODAY?

_____

DATE _____ / _____ / 20 _____

Working hard is important. But there is something that matters even more: believing in yourself.

– HARRY POTTER

I AM GRATEFUL FOR...

_____

WHAT WOULD MAKE TODAY GREAT?

_____

DAILY AFFIRMATION. I AM...

_____

ONE AMAZING THING THAT HAPPENED TODAY

_____

WHAT DID I LEARN TODAY?

_____

DATE ____ / ____ / 20 ____

WORD OF THE DAY: Friend
A person who you like and enjoy being with.
Someone who supports and cares about you.

I AM GRATEFUL FOR...

WHAT WOULD MAKE TODAY GREAT?

DAILY AFFIRMATION. I AM...

ONE AMAZING THING THAT HAPPENED TODAY

WHAT DID I LEARN TODAY?

DATE _____ / _____ / 20 _____

Try to be a rainbow in someone's cloud.
– MAYA ANGELOU

I AM GRATEFUL FOR...

WHAT WOULD MAKE TODAY GREAT?

DAILY AFFIRMATION. I AM...

ONE AMAZING THING THAT HAPPENED TODAY

WHAT DID I LEARN TODAY?

DATE _____ / _____ / 20 _____

················· **CHALLENGE** ·················

Write down all the reasons why you
love your family.

 I AM GRATEFUL FOR...

WHAT WOULD MAKE TODAY GREAT?

DAILY AFFIRMATION. I AM...

 ONE AMAZING THING THAT HAPPENED TODAY

WHAT DID I LEARN TODAY?

DATE _____ / _____ / 20 _____

You are not meant for crawling.
You have wings. Learn to use them.

– RUMI

I AM GRATEFUL FOR...

WHAT WOULD MAKE TODAY GREAT?

DAILY AFFIRMATION. I AM...

ONE AMAZING THING THAT HAPPENED TODAY

WHAT DID I LEARN TODAY?

DATE _____ / _____ / 20 _____

WORD OF THE DAY: Empathy

The feeling that you understand and share
another person's experiences and emotions.

 I AM GRATEFUL FOR...

_____

WHAT WOULD MAKE TODAY GREAT?

_____

DAILY AFFIRMATION. I AM...

_____

ONE AMAZING THING THAT HAPPENED TODAY

_____

WHAT DID I LEARN TODAY?

_____

DATE _____ / _____ / 20 _____

Being different isn't a bad thing. It means
you're brave enough to be yourself.
– LUNA LOVEGOOD (HARRY POTTER)

I AM GRATEFUL FOR...

_____

WHAT WOULD MAKE TODAY GREAT?

_____

DAILY AFFIRMATION. I AM...

_____

ONE AMAZING THING THAT HAPPENED TODAY

_____

WHAT DID I LEARN TODAY?

_____

DATE _____ / _____ / 20 _____

Don't doubt your value. Don't run from who you are.

– C.S. LEWIS

 I AM GRATEFUL FOR...

WHAT WOULD MAKE TODAY GREAT?

DAILY AFFIRMATION. I AM...

 ONE AMAZING THING THAT HAPPENED TODAY

WHAT DID I LEARN TODAY?

DATE _____ / _____ / 20 _____

If you can't feed a hundred people,
then just feed one.

– MOTHER TERESA

I AM GRATEFUL FOR...

_____

WHAT WOULD MAKE TODAY GREAT?

_____

DAILY AFFIRMATION. I AM...

_____

ONE AMAZING THING THAT HAPPENED TODAY

_____

WHAT DID I LEARN TODAY?

_____

DATE _____ / _____ / 20 _____

WORD OF THE DAY: Diligent

Taking care to do a good, thorough job.

 I AM GRATEFUL FOR...

_____

WHAT WOULD MAKE TODAY GREAT?

_____

DAILY AFFIRMATION. I AM...

_____

ONE AMAZING THING THAT HAPPENED TODAY

_____

WHAT DID I LEARN TODAY?

_____

DATE _____ / _____ / 20 _____

CHALLENGE

Read a book with your parents.

I AM GRATEFUL FOR...

WHAT WOULD MAKE TODAY GREAT?

DAILY AFFIRMATION. I AM...

ONE AMAZING THING THAT HAPPENED TODAY

WHAT DID I LEARN TODAY?

DATE _____ / _____ / 20 _____

Time is an illusion, there is only the now.

– MASTER SHIFU (KUNG FU PANDA)

 I AM GRATEFUL FOR...

WHAT WOULD MAKE TODAY GREAT?

DAILY AFFIRMATION. I AM...

ONE AMAZING THING THAT HAPPENED TODAY

WHAT DID I LEARN TODAY?

DATE _____ / _____ / 20 _____

WORD OF THE DAY: Bright
Able to learn things quickly.

I AM GRATEFUL FOR...

WHAT WOULD MAKE TODAY GREAT?

DAILY AFFIRMATION, I AM...

ONE AMAZING THING THAT HAPPENED TODAY

WHAT DID I LEARN TODAY?

DATE ____ / ____ / 20 ____

We must be swift as the coursing river, with all the force of a great typhoon, with all the strength of a raging fire, mysterious as the dark side of a moon.

- SHANG (MULAN)

 I AM GRATEFUL FOR...

WHAT WOULD MAKE TODAY GREAT?

DAILY AFFIRMATION. I AM...

☽ ONE AMAZING THING THAT HAPPENED TODAY

WHAT DID I LEARN TODAY?

DATE _____ / _____ / 20 _____

You have been my friend.
That in itself is a tremendous thing.
—E.B. WHITE, CHARLOTTE'S WEB

I AM GRATEFUL FOR...

WHAT WOULD MAKE TODAY GREAT?

DAILY AFFIRMATION. I AM...

ONE AMAZING THING THAT HAPPENED TODAY

WHAT DID I LEARN TODAY?

DATE _____ / _____ / 20 _____

Books are a uniquely portable magic.
- **STEPHEN KING**

I AM GRATEFUL FOR...

WHAT WOULD MAKE TODAY GREAT?

DAILY AFFIRMATION. I AM...

☾ **ONE AMAZING THING THAT HAPPENED TODAY**

WHAT DID I LEARN TODAY?

DATE _____ / _____ / 20 _____

WORD OF THE DAY: Authentic
Real, genuine, or true.

I AM GRATEFUL FOR...

_____

WHAT WOULD MAKE TODAY GREAT?

_____

DAILY AFFIRMATION, I AM...

_____

ONE AMAZING THING THAT HAPPENED TODAY

_____

WHAT DID I LEARN TODAY?

_____

DATE ____ / ____ / 20 ____

·········· CHALLENGE ··········
Clean your room today.

I AM GRATEFUL FOR...

WHAT WOULD MAKE TODAY GREAT?

DAILY AFFIRMATION. I AM...

ONE AMAZING THING THAT HAPPENED TODAY

WHAT DID I LEARN TODAY?

DATE _____ / _____ / 20 _____

If everyone started off the day singing,
just think how happy they'd be.
- LAUREN MYRACLE

I AM GRATEFUL FOR...

WHAT WOULD MAKE TODAY GREAT?

DAILY AFFIRMATION. I AM...

ONE AMAZING THING THAT HAPPENED TODAY

WHAT DID I LEARN TODAY?

113

DATE _____ / _____ / 20 _____

WORD OF THE DAY: **Calm**

Peaceful and quiet; free from nervousness or anger.

 I AM GRATEFUL FOR...

_____

WHAT WOULD MAKE TODAY GREAT?

_____

DAILY AFFIRMATION. I AM...

_____

ONE AMAZING THING THAT HAPPENED TODAY

_____

WHAT DID I LEARN TODAY?

_____

DATE _____ / _____ / 20 _____

When you learn, teach, when you get, give.
- MAYA ANGELOU

I AM GRATEFUL FOR...

_____

WHAT WOULD MAKE TODAY GREAT?

_____

DAILY AFFIRMATION. I AM...

_____

ONE AMAZING THING THAT HAPPENED TODAY

_____

WHAT DID I LEARN TODAY?

_____

DATE _____ / _____ / 20 _____

Somewhere, something incredible is
waiting to be known.

– SHARON BEGLEY

I AM GRATEFUL FOR...

_____

WHAT WOULD MAKE TODAY GREAT?

_____

DAILY AFFIRMATION. I AM...

_____

ONE AMAZING THING THAT HAPPENED TODAY

_____

WHAT DID I LEARN TODAY?

_____

DATE _____ / _____ / 20 _____

Sing like the birds sing, not worrying about who hears or what they think.

-RUMI

I AM GRATEFUL FOR...

_____

WHAT WOULD MAKE TODAY GREAT?

_____

DAILY AFFIRMATION. I AM...

_____

ONE AMAZING THING THAT HAPPENED TODAY

_____

WHAT DID I LEARN TODAY?

_____

DATE _____ / _____ / 20 _____

WORD OF THE DAY: Benevolent

Desiring to do good and be kind and generous for others.

 I AM GRATEFUL FOR...

WHAT WOULD MAKE TODAY GREAT?

DAILY AFFIRMATION. I AM...

ONE AMAZING THING THAT HAPPENED TODAY

WHAT DID I LEARN TODAY?

DATE _____ / _____ / 20 _____

······· **CHALLENGE** ·······

Watch your favorite movie this week.

I AM GRATEFUL FOR...

_____

WHAT WOULD MAKE TODAY GREAT?

_____

DAILY AFFIRMATION. I AM...

_____

ONE AMAZING THING THAT HAPPENED TODAY

_____

WHAT DID I LEARN TODAY?

_____

DATE _____ / _____ / 20 _____

Even the wisest mind has something yet to learn.

– GEORGE SANTAYANA

I AM GRATEFUL FOR...

WHAT WOULD MAKE TODAY GREAT?

DAILY AFFIRMATION. I AM...

ONE AMAZING THING THAT HAPPENED TODAY

WHAT DID I LEARN TODAY?

DATE _____ / _____ / 20 _____

WORD OF THE DAY: Ingenious

Clever or creative in setting up or working through problems.

I AM GRATEFUL FOR...

WHAT WOULD MAKE TODAY GREAT?

DAILY AFFIRMATION. I AM...

ONE AMAZING THING THAT HAPPENED TODAY

WHAT DID I LEARN TODAY?

DATE _____ / _____ / 20 _____

Anyone who stops learning is old, whether at twenty or eighty. Anyone who keeps learning stays young.

– HENRY FORD

I AM GRATEFUL FOR...

WHAT WOULD MAKE TODAY GREAT?

DAILY AFFIRMATION. I AM...

ONE AMAZING THING THAT HAPPENED TODAY

WHAT DID I LEARN TODAY?

DATE _____ / _____ / 20 _____

Success is not final, failure is not fatal:
it is the courage to continue that counts.
— WINSTON S. CHURCHILL

I AM GRATEFUL FOR...

_____

WHAT WOULD MAKE TODAY GREAT?

_____

DAILY AFFIRMATION. I AM...

_____

ONE AMAZING THING THAT HAPPENED TODAY

_____

WHAT DID I LEARN TODAY?

_____

DATE _____ / _____ / 20 _____

To laugh at yourself is to love yourself.
–MICKEY MOUSE

 I AM GRATEFUL FOR...

_____

WHAT WOULD MAKE TODAY GREAT?

_____

DAILY AFFIRMATION. I AM...

_____

ONE AMAZING THING THAT HAPPENED TODAY

_____

WHAT DID I LEARN TODAY?

_____

DATE _____ / _____ / 20 _____

WORD OF THE DAY: Persistent
Continuing to do something or to try
to do something even though it is difficult.

I AM GRATEFUL FOR...

WHAT WOULD MAKE TODAY GREAT?

DAILY AFFIRMATION, I AM...

ONE AMAZING THING THAT HAPPENED TODAY

WHAT DID I LEARN TODAY?

DATE _____ / _____ / 20 _____

.... CHALLENGE ....
Focus on your breathe by counting 10 inhales and 10
exhales in a row. Do this again, next time you feel upset.
....

  I AM GRATEFUL FOR...

WHAT WOULD MAKE TODAY GREAT?

DAILY AFFIRMATION. I AM...

ONE AMAZING THING THAT HAPPENED TODAY

WHAT DID I LEARN TODAY?

126

DATE _____ / _____ / 20 _____

The meaning of life is to find your gift.
The purpose of life is to give it away

– DAVID VISCOTT

I AM GRATEFUL FOR...

WHAT WOULD MAKE TODAY GREAT?

DAILY AFFIRMATION. I AM...

ONE AMAZING THING THAT HAPPENED TODAY

WHAT DID I LEARN TODAY?

DATE _____ / _____ / 20 _____

WORD OF THE DAY: Proactive

Preparing for a situation by making things happen rather than reacting to it.

 I AM GRATEFUL FOR...

_____

WHAT WOULD MAKE TODAY GREAT?

_____

DAILY AFFIRMATION. I AM...

_____

ONE AMAZING THING THAT HAPPENED TODAY

_____

WHAT DID I LEARN TODAY?

_____

DATE _____ / _____ / 20 _____

Do what you can, with what you have,
where you are.

THEODORE ROOSEVELT

I AM GRATEFUL FOR...

WHAT WOULD MAKE TODAY GREAT?

DAILY AFFIRMATION. I AM...

ONE AMAZING THING THAT HAPPENED TODAY

WHAT DID I LEARN TODAY?

DATE _____ / _____ / 20 _____

Think of giving not as a duty,
but as a privilege.

– JOHN D. ROCKEFELLER

 I AM GRATEFUL FOR...

WHAT WOULD MAKE TODAY GREAT?

DAILY AFFIRMATION. I AM...

ONE AMAZING THING THAT HAPPENED TODAY

WHAT DID I LEARN TODAY?

DATE _____ / _____ / 20 _____

Today's special moments are tomorrow's memories

– GENIE (ALADDIN 2)

I AM GRATEFUL FOR...

_____

WHAT WOULD MAKE TODAY GREAT?

_____

DAILY AFFIRMATION. I AM...

_____

ONE AMAZING THING THAT HAPPENED TODAY

_____

WHAT DID I LEARN TODAY?

_____

DATE _____ / _____ / 20 _____

WORD OF THE DAY: **Efficient**

Working in an organized way without
wasting materials, time, or energy.

I AM GRATEFUL FOR...

_____

WHAT WOULD MAKE TODAY GREAT?

_____

DAILY AFFIRMATION. I AM...

_____

ONE AMAZING THING THAT HAPPENED TODAY

_____

WHAT DID I LEARN TODAY?

_____

DATE _____ / _____ / 20 _____

··· CHALLENGE ···

Get outside today and go play!

I AM GRATEFUL FOR...

WHAT WOULD MAKE TODAY GREAT?

DAILY AFFIRMATION. I AM...

ONE AMAZING THING THAT HAPPENED TODAY

WHAT DID I LEARN TODAY?

DATE _____ / _____ / 20 _____

*True humility is not thinking less of yourself;
it is thinking of yourself less.*

– C.S. LEWIS

 I AM GRATEFUL FOR...

WHAT WOULD MAKE TODAY GREAT?

DAILY AFFIRMATION. I AM...

 ONE AMAZING THING THAT HAPPENED TODAY

WHAT DID I LEARN TODAY?

DATE _____ / _____ / 20 _____

WORD OF THE DAY: Fearless

Not afraid; very brave.

I AM GRATEFUL FOR...

WHAT WOULD MAKE TODAY GREAT?

DAILY AFFIRMATION. I AM...

ONE AMAZING THING THAT HAPPENED TODAY

WHAT DID I LEARN TODAY?

DATE _____ / _____ / 20 _____

Whatever you are, be a good one.
– ABRAHAM LINCOLN

 I AM GRATEFUL FOR...

_____

WHAT WOULD MAKE TODAY GREAT?

_____

DAILY AFFIRMATION. I AM...

_____

 ONE AMAZING THING THAT HAPPENED TODAY

_____

WHAT DID I LEARN TODAY?

_____

DATE _____ / _____ / 20 _____

The best preparation for tomorrow is doing your best today.

— H. JACKSON BROWN

I AM GRATEFUL FOR...

_____

WHAT WOULD MAKE TODAY GREAT?

_____

DAILY AFFIRMATION. I AM...

_____

ONE AMAZING THING THAT HAPPENED TODAY

_____

WHAT DID I LEARN TODAY?

_____

DATE _____ / _____ / 20 _____

*If your actions inspire others to dream more,
learn more, do more and become more,
you are a leader.*

– JOHN QUINCY ADAMS

 I AM GRATEFUL FOR...

_____

WHAT WOULD MAKE TODAY GREAT?

_____

DAILY AFFIRMATION. I AM...

_____

 ONE AMAZING THING THAT HAPPENED TODAY

_____

WHAT DID I LEARN TODAY?

_____

DATE ___ / ___ / 20 ___

WORD OF THE DAY: Generous

Showing kindness for others; giving more
than what is expected.

I AM GRATEFUL FOR...

WHAT WOULD MAKE TODAY GREAT?

DAILY AFFIRMATION. I AM...

ONE AMAZING THING THAT HAPPENED TODAY

WHAT DID I LEARN TODAY?

DATE _____ / _____ / 20 _____

CHALLENGE
Give your mom and/or dad a big hug today.

☀ I AM GRATEFUL FOR...

WHAT WOULD MAKE TODAY GREAT?

DAILY AFFIRMATION. I AM...

ONE AMAZING THING THAT HAPPENED TODAY

WHAT DID I LEARN TODAY?

DATE _____ / _____ / 20 _____

Everything is awesome!
- LEGO MOVIE

I AM GRATEFUL FOR...

WHAT WOULD MAKE TODAY GREAT?

DAILY AFFIRMATION. I AM...

ONE AMAZING THING THAT HAPPENED TODAY

WHAT DID I LEARN TODAY?

M!

DATE _____ / _____ / 20 _____

WORD OF THE DAY: Devoted

Having strong love or loyalty for something
or someone.

 I AM GRATEFUL FOR...

WHAT WOULD MAKE TODAY GREAT?

DAILY AFFIRMATION. I AM...

ONE AMAZING THING THAT HAPPENED TODAY

WHAT DID I LEARN TODAY?

DATE ———— / ———— / 20 ————

A warm smile is the universal
language of kindness.
- WILLIAM ARTHUR WARD

I AM GRATEFUL FOR...

WHAT WOULD MAKE TODAY GREAT?

DAILY AFFIRMATION. I AM...

ONE AMAZING THING THAT HAPPENED TODAY

WHAT DID I LEARN TODAY?

DATE ___ / ___ / 20 ___

Always be a little kinder than necessary.
-JAMES M. BARRIE

I AM GRATEFUL FOR...

WHAT WOULD MAKE TODAY GREAT?

DAILY AFFIRMATION. I AM...

ONE AMAZING THING THAT HAPPENED TODAY

WHAT DID I LEARN TODAY?

141

DATE ———— / ———— / 20 ————

Oh yes, the past can hurt...but you either run from it, OR learn from it.
—RAFIKI (THE LION KING)

I AM GRATEFUL FOR...

———————————————————————————

WHAT WOULD MAKE TODAY GREAT?

———————————————————————————

DAILY AFFIRMATION. I AM...

———————————————————————————

ONE AMAZING THING THAT HAPPENED TODAY

———————————————————————————

WHAT DID I LEARN TODAY?

———————————————————————————

145

DATE _____ / _____ / 20 _____

WORD OF THE DAY: Exuberant

Very lively, happy, or energetic; filled with energy and enthusiasm.

 I AM GRATEFUL FOR...

WHAT WOULD MAKE TODAY GREAT?

DAILY AFFIRMATION. I AM...

 ONE AMAZING THING THAT HAPPENED TODAY

WHAT DID I LEARN TODAY?

DATE _____ / _____ / 20 _____

················· CHALLENGE ·················

Take a really silly picture today.

I AM GRATEFUL FOR...

WHAT WOULD MAKE TODAY GREAT?

DAILY AFFIRMATION. I AM...

ONE AMAZING THING THAT HAPPENED TODAY

WHAT DID I LEARN TODAY?

DATE _____ / _____ / 20 _____

Reach high, for stars lie hidden in your soul.
Dream deep, for every dream precedes the goal.

— PAMELA VAULL STARR

I AM GRATEFUL FOR...

WHAT WOULD MAKE TODAY GREAT?

DAILY AFFIRMATION. I AM...

ONE AMAZING THING THAT HAPPENED TODAY

WHAT DID I LEARN TODAY?

DATE _____ / _____ / 20 _____

WORD OF THE DAY: Eager

Feeling a strong and impatient desire to do something or to have something; very excited and interested.

I AM GRATEFUL FOR...

_____

WHAT WOULD MAKE TODAY GREAT?

_____

DAILY AFFIRMATION. I AM...

_____

ONE AMAZING THING THAT HAPPENED TODAY

_____

WHAT DID I LEARN TODAY?

_____

DATE ____ / ____ / 20 ____

You cannot open a book without
learning something.
- CONFUCIOUS

I AM GRATEFUL FOR...

_____

WHAT WOULD MAKE TODAY GREAT?

_____

DAILY AFFIRMATION. I AM...

_____

ONE AMAZING THING THAT HAPPENED TODAY

_____

WHAT DID I LEARN TODAY?

_____

150

DATE ____ / ____ / 20 ____

The secret of leadership is simple: Do what you believe in. Paint a picture of the future. Go there. People will follow.

- SETH GODIN

I AM GRATEFUL FOR...

WHAT WOULD MAKE TODAY GREAT?

DAILY AFFIRMATION. I AM...

ONE AMAZING THING THAT HAPPENED TODAY

WHAT DID I LEARN TODAY?

151

DATE _____ / _____ / 20 _____

Luck is what happens
when preparation meets opportunity.
-SENECA

I AM GRATEFUL FOR...

WHAT WOULD MAKE TODAY GREAT?

DAILY AFFIRMATION. I AM...

ONE AMAZING THING THAT HAPPENED TODAY

WHAT DID I LEARN TODAY?

DATE ____ / ____ / 20 ____

WORD OF THE DAY: **Spirited**

Full of courage or energy; very lively or determined.

I AM GRATEFUL FOR...

_____

WHAT WOULD MAKE TODAY GREAT?

_____

DAILY AFFIRMATION. I AM...

_____

ONE AMAZING THING THAT HAPPENED TODAY

_____

WHAT DID I LEARN TODAY?

_____

154

WHAT DID I LEARN TODAY?

 ONE AMAZING THING THAT HAPPENED TODAY

DAILY AFFIRMATION. I AM...

WHAT WOULD MAKE TODAY GREAT?

 I AM GRATEFUL FOR...

.... CHALLENGE ....
Give your teacher a compliment today.

DATE ____ / ____ / 20 ____

DATE _____ / _____ / 20 _____

I am not what happened to me.
I am what I choose to become.
-CARL JUNG-

I AM GRATEFUL FOR...

WHAT WOULD MAKE TODAY GREAT?

DAILY AFFIRMATION. I AM...

ONE AMAZING THING THAT HAPPENED TODAY

WHAT DID I LEARN TODAY?

DATE _____ / _____ / 20 _____

WORD OF THE DAY: **Tough**

To deal with a difficult situation
by being determined and strong.

I AM GRATEFUL FOR...

_____

WHAT WOULD MAKE TODAY GREAT?

_____

DAILY AFFIRMATION. I AM...

_____

ONE AMAZING THING THAT HAPPENED TODAY

_____

WHAT DID I LEARN TODAY?

_____

DATE _____ / _____ / 20 _____

We do not need magic to transform our world.
We carry all of the power we need inside
ourselves already.

-J.K. ROWLING

I AM GRATEFUL FOR...

WHAT WOULD MAKE TODAY GREAT?

DAILY AFFIRMATION. I AM...

ONE AMAZING THING THAT HAPPENED TODAY

WHAT DID I LEARN TODAY?

DATE _____ / _____ / 20 _____

If we wait until we're ready, we'll be waiting for the rest of our lives.

-LEMONY SNICKET

I AM GRATEFUL FOR...

WHAT WOULD MAKE TODAY GREAT?

DAILY AFFIRMATION. I AM...

ONE AMAZING THING THAT HAPPENED TODAY

WHAT DID I LEARN TODAY?

DATE _____ / _____ / 20 _____

Everything is possible. The impossible just takes longer.
-DAN BROWN

I AM GRATEFUL FOR...

_____

WHAT WOULD MAKE TODAY GREAT?

_____

DAILY AFFIRMATION. I AM...

_____

ONE AMAZING THING THAT HAPPENED TODAY

_____

WHAT DID I LEARN TODAY?

_____

DATE ———— / ———— / 20 ————

WORD OF THE DAY: Open-Minded
Willing to consider different ideas or opinions.

 I AM GRATEFUL FOR...

___

WHAT WOULD MAKE TODAY GREAT?

___

DAILY AFFIRMATION. I AM...

___

ONE AMAZING THING THAT HAPPENED TODAY

___

WHAT DID I LEARN TODAY?

___

DATE ____ / ____ / 20 ____

---- CHALLENGE ----
If you started a business, what would it be?

I AM GRATEFUL FOR...

WHAT WOULD MAKE TODAY GREAT?

DAILY AFFIRMATION. I AM...

ONE AMAZING THING THAT HAPPENED TODAY

WHAT DID I LEARN TODAY?

161

DATE _____ / _____ / 20 _____

Nurture your mind with great thoughts.
To believe in the heroic makes heroes.

-BENJAMIN DISRAELI

 I AM GRATEFUL FOR...

_____

WHAT WOULD MAKE TODAY GREAT?

_____

DAILY AFFIRMATION. I AM...

_____

 ONE AMAZING THING THAT HAPPENED TODAY

_____

WHAT DID I LEARN TODAY?

_____

DATE _____ / _____ / 20 _____

WORD OF THE DAY: **Introspection**

The process of examining your own thoughts or feelings.

I AM GRATEFUL FOR...

_____

WHAT WOULD MAKE TODAY GREAT?

_____

DAILY AFFIRMATION. I AM...

_____

ONE AMAZING THING THAT HAPPENED TODAY

_____

WHAT DID I LEARN TODAY?

_____

DATE _____ / _____ / 20 _____

Ever tried. Ever failed. No matter.
Try again. Fail again. Fail better.
-SAMUEL BECKETT

 I AM GRATEFUL FOR...

WHAT WOULD MAKE TODAY GREAT?

DAILY AFFIRMATION. I AM...

 ONE AMAZING THING THAT HAPPENED TODAY

WHAT DID I LEARN TODAY?

DATE _____ / _____ / 20 _____

You can't depend on your eyes
when your imagination is out of focus.
-MARK TWAIN

I AM GRATEFUL FOR...

_____

WHAT WOULD MAKE TODAY GREAT?

_____

DAILY AFFIRMATION. I AM...

_____

ONE AMAZING THING THAT HAPPENED TODAY

_____

WHAT DID I LEARN TODAY?

_____

DATE _____ / _____ / 20 _____

Spread love everywhere you go. Let no one ever come to you without leaving happier.

-MOTHER TERESA

 I AM GRATEFUL FOR...

_____

WHAT WOULD MAKE TODAY GREAT?

_____

DAILY AFFIRMATION. I AM...

_____

ONE AMAZING THING THAT HAPPENED TODAY

_____

WHAT DID I LEARN TODAY?

_____

DATE _____ / _____ / 20 _____

WORD OF THE DAY: Joyful

Feeling, causing, or showing great happiness.

I AM GRATEFUL FOR...

_____

WHAT WOULD MAKE TODAY GREAT?

_____

DAILY AFFIRMATION. I AM...

_____

ONE AMAZING THING THAT HAPPENED TODAY

_____

WHAT DID I LEARN TODAY?

_____

DATE _____ / _____ / 20 _____

························· **CHALLENGE** ·························

Ask your parents if there is any household
chore you can help with today.

 I AM GRATEFUL FOR...

_____

WHAT WOULD MAKE TODAY GREAT?

_____

DAILY AFFIRMATION. I AM...

_____

ONE AMAZING THING THAT HAPPENED TODAY

_____

WHAT DID I LEARN TODAY?

_____

DATE _____ / _____ / 20 _____

I didn't lose the gold. I won the silver.

-MICHELLE KWAN

I AM GRATEFUL FOR...

_____

WHAT WOULD MAKE TODAY GREAT?

_____

DAILY AFFIRMATION. I AM...

_____

ONE AMAZING THING THAT HAPPENED TODAY

_____

WHAT DID I LEARN TODAY?

_____

DATE _____ / _____ / 20 _____

WORD OF THE DAY: **Observant**

Good at watching and listening; good at noticing what is going on around you.

 I AM GRATEFUL FOR...

_____

WHAT WOULD MAKE TODAY GREAT?

_____

DAILY AFFIRMATION. I AM...

_____

ONE AMAZING THING THAT HAPPENED TODAY

_____

WHAT DID I LEARN TODAY?

_____

DATE _____ / _____ / 20 _____

A ship is safe in harbor, but that's not what ships are for.

-JOHN A. SHEDD

I AM GRATEFUL FOR...

_____

WHAT WOULD MAKE TODAY GREAT?

_____

DAILY AFFIRMATION. I AM...

_____

ONE AMAZING THING THAT HAPPENED TODAY

_____

WHAT DID I LEARN TODAY?

_____

DATE _____ / _____ / 20 _____

You bring out the best in yourself by
looking for the best in others.

-GENE BEDLEY

I AM GRATEFUL FOR...

WHAT WOULD MAKE TODAY GREAT?

DAILY AFFIRMATION. I AM...

ONE AMAZING THING THAT HAPPENED TODAY

WHAT DID I LEARN TODAY?

DATE _____ / _____ / 20 _____

For the strength of the pack is the wolf,
and the strength of the wolf is the pack.

RUDYARD KIPLING

I AM GRATEFUL FOR...

_____

WHAT WOULD MAKE TODAY GREAT?

_____

DAILY AFFIRMATION. I AM...

_____

ONE AMAZING THING THAT HAPPENED TODAY

_____

WHAT DID I LEARN TODAY?

_____

DATE _____ / _____ / 20 _____

WORD OF THE DAY: **Enthusiastic**

Feeling or showing strong excitement about something.

 I AM GRATEFUL FOR...

WHAT WOULD MAKE TODAY GREAT?

DAILY AFFIRMATION. I AM...

ONE AMAZING THING THAT HAPPENED TODAY

WHAT DID I LEARN TODAY?

DATE ____ / ____ / 20 ____

---- CHALLENGE ----
Sing your favorite song today.

I AM GRATEFUL FOR…

WHAT WOULD MAKE TODAY GREAT?

DAILY AFFIRMATION. I AM…

ONE AMAZING THING THAT HAPPENED TODAY

WHAT DID I LEARN TODAY?

175

DATE ———/———/ 20 ———

It's not that I'm smart. It's that I stay with problems longer.
-ALBERT EINSTEIN

I AM GRATEFUL FOR...

WHAT WOULD MAKE TODAY GREAT?

DAILY AFFIRMATION. I AM...

ONE AMAZING THING THAT HAPPENED TODAY

WHAT DID I LEARN TODAY?

DATE _____ / _____ / 20 _____

WORD OF THE DAY: Independent

Acting or thinking freely instead of being guided by other people.

I AM GRATEFUL FOR...

_____

WHAT WOULD MAKE TODAY GREAT?

_____

DAILY AFFIRMATION. I AM...

_____

ONE AMAZING THING THAT HAPPENED TODAY

_____

WHAT DID I LEARN TODAY?

_____

DATE _____ / _____ / 20 _____

Start where you are. Use what you have.
Do what you can.
-ARTHUR ASHE

 I AM GRATEFUL FOR...

_____

WHAT WOULD MAKE TODAY GREAT?

_____

DAILY AFFIRMATION. I AM...

_____

ONE AMAZING THING THAT HAPPENED TODAY

_____

WHAT DID I LEARN TODAY?

_____

DATE _____ / _____ / 20 _____

Enjoy the little things in life for one day you'll look back and realize they were the big things.
-KURT VONNEGUT

I AM GRATEFUL FOR...

WHAT WOULD MAKE TODAY GREAT?

DAILY AFFIRMATION. I AM...

ONE AMAZING THING THAT HAPPENED TODAY

WHAT DID I LEARN TODAY?

DATE _____ / _____ / 20 _____

The happiness of your life depends upon
the quality of your thoughts.

-MARCUS AURELIUS

I AM GRATEFUL FOR...

WHAT WOULD MAKE TODAY GREAT?

DAILY AFFIRMATION. I AM...

ONE AMAZING THING THAT HAPPENED TODAY

WHAT DID I LEARN TODAY?

DATE _____ / _____ / 20 _____

WORD OF THE DAY: Captivating

Attractive and interesting in a way that holds your attention.

I AM GRATEFUL FOR...

WHAT WOULD MAKE TODAY GREAT?

DAILY AFFIRMATION, I AM...

ONE AMAZING THING THAT HAPPENED TODAY

WHAT DID I LEARN TODAY?

DATE ____/____/ 20 ____

-------- CHALLENGE --------
Sit in silence with your eyes closed for 5
minutes today. What did you observe?

 I AM GRATEFUL FOR...

_____

WHAT WOULD MAKE TODAY GREAT?

_____

DAILY AFFIRMATION. I AM...

_____

ONE AMAZING THING THAT HAPPENED TODAY

_____

WHAT DID I LEARN TODAY?

_____

DATE _____ / _____ / 20 _____

The more we do, the more we can do.
—WILLIAM HAZLITT

I AM GRATEFUL FOR...

_____

WHAT WOULD MAKE TODAY GREAT?

_____

DAILY AFFIRMATION. I AM...

_____

ONE AMAZING THING THAT HAPPENED TODAY

_____

WHAT DID I LEARN TODAY?

_____

183

DATE _____ / _____ / 20 _____

WORD OF THE DAY: **Unique**

Something or someone who is unlike
anything or anyone else.

 I AM GRATEFUL FOR...

_____

WHAT WOULD MAKE TODAY GREAT?

_____

DAILY AFFIRMATION. I AM...

_____

 ONE AMAZING THING THAT HAPPENED TODAY

_____

WHAT DID I LEARN TODAY?

_____

DATE _____ / _____ / 20 _____

Fall seven times, stand up eight.
—JAPANESE PROVERB

I AM GRATEFUL FOR...

_____

WHAT WOULD MAKE TODAY GREAT?

_____

DAILY AFFIRMATION. I AM...

_____

ONE AMAZING THING THAT HAPPENED TODAY

_____

WHAT DID I LEARN TODAY?

_____

185

DATE _____ / _____ / 20 _____

We must be the change we wish
to see in our world.
-MAHATMA GANDHI

 I AM GRATEFUL FOR...

WHAT WOULD MAKE TODAY GREAT?

DAILY AFFIRMATION. I AM...

ONE AMAZING THING THAT HAPPENED TODAY

WHAT DID I LEARN TODAY?

DATE ____ / ____ / 20 ____

WORD OF THE DAY: **Thoughtfulness**

Considering the needs or feelings of other people.

I AM GRATEFUL FOR...

WHAT WOULD MAKE TODAY GREAT?

DAILY AFFIRMATION. I AM...

ONE AMAZING THING THAT HAPPENED TODAY

WHAT DID I LEARN TODAY?

187

DATE _____ / _____ / 20 _____

How does one become a butterfly? You must want to fly so much that you are willing to give up being a caterpillar.

-TRINA PAULUS

I AM GRATEFUL FOR...

_____

WHAT WOULD MAKE TODAY GREAT?

_____

DAILY AFFIRMATION. I AM...

_____

 ONE AMAZING THING THAT HAPPENED TODAY

_____

WHAT DID I LEARN TODAY?

_____

DATE _____ / _____ / 20 _____

.... **CHALLENGE** ....
Write a letter to your future self.
....

I AM GRATEFUL FOR...

_____

WHAT WOULD MAKE TODAY GREAT?

_____

DAILY AFFIRMATION. I AM...

_____

ONE AMAZING THING THAT HAPPENED TODAY

_____

WHAT DID I LEARN TODAY?

_____

DATE _____ / _____ / 20 _____

Stop asking what others can do for us, and start asking what we can do for others.
—AUSTIN KLEON

I AM GRATEFUL FOR…

_____

WHAT WOULD MAKE TODAY GREAT?

_____

DAILY AFFIRMATION. I AM…

_____

ONE AMAZING THING THAT HAPPENED TODAY

_____

WHAT DID I LEARN TODAY?

_____

DATE _____ / _____ / 20 _____

WORD OF THE DAY: **Protect**

To keep someone or something safe.

I AM GRATEFUL FOR...

WHAT WOULD MAKE TODAY GREAT?

DAILY AFFIRMATION. I AM...

ONE AMAZING THING THAT HAPPENED TODAY

WHAT DID I LEARN TODAY?

DATE _____ / _____ / 20 _____

The best way to improve your self-control
is to see how and why you lose control.
-KELLY MCGONIGAL

 I AM GRATEFUL FOR...

WHAT WOULD MAKE TODAY GREAT?

DAILY AFFIRMATION. I AM...

 ONE AMAZING THING THAT HAPPENED TODAY

WHAT DID I LEARN TODAY?

DATE _____ / _____ / 20 _____

Personal success is when you work your
hardest to become your best.

-JOHN WOODEN

I AM GRATEFUL FOR...

WHAT WOULD MAKE TODAY GREAT?

DAILY AFFIRMATION. I AM...

ONE AMAZING THING THAT HAPPENED TODAY

WHAT DID I LEARN TODAY?

DATE _____ / _____ / 20 _____

Count your age by friends, not years.
Count your life by smiles, not tears.

-DIXIE WILLSON

I AM GRATEFUL FOR...

WHAT WOULD MAKE TODAY GREAT?

DAILY AFFIRMATION. I AM...

ONE AMAZING THING THAT HAPPENED TODAY

WHAT DID I LEARN TODAY?

DATE _____ / _____ / 20 _____

WORD OF THE DAY: Courteous
Very polite in a way that shows respect.

I AM GRATEFUL FOR...

_____

WHAT WOULD MAKE TODAY GREAT?

_____

DAILY AFFIRMATION, I AM...

_____

ONE AMAZING THING THAT HAPPENED TODAY

_____

WHAT DID I LEARN TODAY?

_____

You have two weeks of the journal left to complete.

Now's the time to order your next journal to make sure you don't miss a day of journaling! Check out *www.fiveminutejournalforkids.com* for more information.

DATE ____ / ____ / 20 ____

.... CHALLENGE ....
Write your parents an encouraging note today.
....

I AM GRATEFUL FOR...

WHAT WOULD MAKE TODAY GREAT?

DAILY AFFIRMATION. I AM...

ONE AMAZING THING THAT HAPPENED TODAY

WHAT DID I LEARN TODAY?

DATE ____ / ____ / 20 ____

The most sophisticated people I know – inside they are all children.
—JIM HENSON

I AM GRATEFUL FOR...

WHAT WOULD MAKE TODAY GREAT?

DAILY AFFIRMATION. I AM...

ONE AMAZING THING THAT HAPPENED TODAY

WHAT DID I LEARN TODAY?

DATE ____ / ____ / 20 ____

WORD OF THE DAY: Honorable
Having or showing honesty and good
moral character.

I AM GRATEFUL FOR...

_____

WHAT WOULD MAKE TODAY GREAT?

_____

DAILY AFFIRMATION. I AM...

_____

ONE AMAZING THING THAT HAPPENED TODAY

_____

WHAT DID I LEARN TODAY?

_____

199

DATE _____ / _____ / 20 _____

Sometimes me think, 'What is Friend?' and then
me say, 'Friend is someone to share
the last cookie with'.

-COOKIE MONSTER

I AM GRATEFUL FOR...

WHAT WOULD MAKE TODAY GREAT?

DAILY AFFIRMATION. I AM...

ONE AMAZING THING THAT HAPPENED TODAY

WHAT DID I LEARN TODAY?

DATE _____ / _____ / 20 _____

Consider everything an experiment.
-CORITA KENT-

I AM GRATEFUL FOR...

WHAT WOULD MAKE TODAY GREAT?

DAILY AFFIRMATION. I AM...

ONE AMAZING THING THAT HAPPENED TODAY

WHAT DID I LEARN TODAY?

DATE _____ / _____ / 20 _____

When you establish peace, when you etablish
love, when you establish kindness here
[inside], you cannot act any other way
to the outside world.

-MIMI IKONN

 I AM GRATEFUL FOR...

_____

WHAT WOULD MAKE TODAY GREAT?

_____

DAILY AFFIRMATION. I AM...

_____

ONE AMAZING THING THAT HAPPENED TODAY

_____

WHAT DID I LEARN TODAY?

_____

DATE _____ / _____ / 20 _____

WORD OF THE DAY: Tolerance

Willingness to accept feelings, habits, or beliefs that are different from your own.

I AM GRATEFUL FOR...

_____

WHAT WOULD MAKE TODAY GREAT?

_____

DAILY AFFIRMATION. I AM...

_____

ONE AMAZING THING THAT HAPPENED TODAY

_____

WHAT DID I LEARN TODAY?

_____

DATE _____ / _____ / 20 _____

CHALLENGE

Enjoy next Saturday or Sunday
without any electronic devices.

I AM GRATEFUL FOR...

WHAT WOULD MAKE TODAY GREAT?

DAILY AFFIRMATION. I AM...

ONE AMAZING THING THAT HAPPENED TODAY

WHAT DID I LEARN TODAY?

DATE _____ / _____ / 20 _____

> Laugh my friend, for laughter ignites a fire within the pit of your belly and awakens your being.
>
> -STELLA MCCARTNEY

I AM GRATEFUL FOR...

___

WHAT WOULD MAKE TODAY GREAT?

___

DAILY AFFIRMATION. I AM...

___

ONE AMAZING THING THAT HAPPENED TODAY

___

WHAT DID I LEARN TODAY?

___

DATE _____ / _____ / 20 _____

WORD OF THE DAY: Sentimental

Prompted by feelings of tenderness,
sadness, or nostalgia.

I AM GRATEFUL FOR...

_____

WHAT WOULD MAKE TODAY GREAT?

_____

DAILY AFFIRMATION, I AM...

_____

ONE AMAZING THING THAT HAPPENED TODAY

_____

WHAT DID I LEARN TODAY?

_____

DATE _____ / _____ / _____ 20 _____

What we know matters, but who
we are matters more.
-BRENÉ BROWN

I AM GRATEFUL FOR...

_____

WHAT WOULD MAKE TODAY GREAT?

_____

DAILY AFFIRMATION. I AM...

_____

ONE AMAZING THING THAT HAPPENED TODAY

_____

WHAT DID I LEARN TODAY?

_____

DATE _____ / _____ / 20 _____

It's no use going back to yesterday,
because I was a different person then.

-LEWIS CAROLL

I AM GRATEFUL FOR...

_____

WHAT WOULD MAKE TODAY GREAT?

_____

DAILY AFFIRMATION. I AM...

_____

 ONE AMAZING THING THAT HAPPENED TODAY

_____

WHAT DID I LEARN TODAY?

_____

DATE _____ / _____ / 20 _____

Mistakes are always forgivable,
if one has the courage to admit them.
-BRUCE LEE

I AM GRATEFUL FOR...

_____

WHAT WOULD MAKE TODAY GREAT?

_____

DAILY AFFIRMATION. I AM...

_____

ONE AMAZING THING THAT HAPPENED TODAY

_____

WHAT DID I LEARN TODAY?

_____

Woo hoo! Way to go!

Congratulations! You have just finished 6 months worth of journaling!

Now, take a deep breath, smile, and rest a few moments to celebrate this milestone. Milestones are events that mark a stage of learning and development. It's a great time to reflect on how far you have come.

You pushed past the days you were cozy in bed and did not feel like writing. You expanded your vocabulary. You bravely took on new challenges.

Bravo on committing to your Five Minute Journal and becoming an even better you. *Please enjoy this milestone by celebrating!*

Ready to start your next journaling journey? If you have not done so already, you can get your next Five Minute Journal for Kids at www.fiveminutejournalforkids.com